An Exercise That

Eliminates Negatives In Your Life

And

Helps You Build A Better Relationship With God

By

Michael Cook

God Is...

An Exercise That Eliminates Negatives in Your Life And Helps You Build A Better Relationship With God.

Copyright 2010 © by J Michael Cook

All rights reserved. No part of this book may be reproduced or transmitted in any form or by any means, electronic or mechanical, including photocopying, except for the inclusion of brief quotations in a review, without permission in writing from the author.

Published by The Michaels Group
Austin, Texas.

Printed in the United States of America
ISBN
978-0-9844485-0-0

The Cover photograph is The Helix Nebula also called the Gods Eye Nebula. Credit: NASA, ESA, C.R.O'Dell (Vanderbuilt University), M.Meixner and P. McCullogh (STSci).

http://hubblesite.org/

Introduction

A few years ago I was experiencing some negatives in my life. As a student of Metaphysics I was very clear of the fact that God gave us the ability to create reality in our lives. I was also clear that it is just as easy to create negative circumstances in your life as it is to create positive circumstances. After all, God gave us the free will to create our own lives.

The solution to ridding myself of the negatives was simple; just quit thinking the negative thoughts. Well, as we all know, that is easier said than done. Over a period of about a month I developed a system that worked to make the negatives leave my mind and my life forever. Over the years I have shared <u>God Is..</u> with friends, some have passed it on to their friends. I am happy to report that it has made significant differences in some people's lives. Now it is time for me to share my system with the world.

My goal is to give you something to think about, hopefully for the rest of your life. My hope is that my ideas, my vision, will cause you to use <u>your</u> mind to consider what I say, but to draw your own lessons and conclusions.

In this book I use the term God, however, He/She can be called by many names: Allah, The IS, the Divine Mind, and The Force, to name a few. God is referred to as He in this text, however, God is both genders: He and She.

The book is an exercise and there are pages available for you to write down your thoughts.

4

Explanation

The realization that God exists is the defining moment in your life, the single most important realization of your life. Why? Because you understand that there is a higher power and you are not in this lifetime alone. This is the most important concept for us to grasp. I cannot prove to you that God exists. Proof of God exists with experience. I can share my experiences, and my faith, but you must have your own experience to know that God IS. You must have your own idea, your own concept, and your own vision of the God you believe in. Your truth! One way to gain that experience is by building your relationship with God.

My concept, my vision, my truth is not relevant to you. Neither are the concepts offered by any of the religions. What is important is the <u>truth</u> that you discover in your search, the vision that you hold in your mind and in your heart. This is <u>your</u> Relationship, the most import Relationship you'll ever have so it must be accepted as truth in your heart and mind. You must not have any doubt in your belief. You must have faith in your belief.

6

Who is God? What is God? These are important questions for anyone seeking truth and purpose in their lives.

It says in the Bible that God created us in His image. What does that mean? Does that mean God looks like me? Does God look like you? Man, woman, black, white, tall, short? He can't look like all of us. Doesn't make much sense does it?

God is energy, pure energy. We ARE created in God's image. In fact, we are created from God's energy. What God created was our souls, and our souls live forever. God is at the center of everything. We all have our own identity, our own consciousness, our own self-awareness; we all vibrate at our own individual frequency. We are created equally but no two of us are the same. Do not confuse being created equally and being born equally. We are not born into equal circumstances.

Believing in God is not enough. You need to establish a relationship with God. God is always there, always willing to have this relationship with you but you must try to communicate. You must be open to communication. What kind of God do you expect? Do you expect the vengeful God depicted in the Old Testament? Do you expect a loving God? Do you blame God for the negatives in your life and take personal credit for all the good in your life?

Each of us is responsible for opening the communication channel with God. This is the Prime Human Directive. God is already there, within you, waiting for you to open the channel and to call upon His power and His love.

In fact, God speaks to everyone. However, until you open that channel on your receiver you are not hearing Him or receiving His guidance. If you believe that it is impossible to reach God, then the odds are you never will because you will not try. God is not withholding Himself from you. You are trying to limit God by believing you cannot reach Him. If you believe that you can reach God and you try, you <u>will</u> reach God and your life will start changing from this point.

God gave us many abilities; the most important to understand and develop is the ability to create your own reality, your world, your existence, and your personal drama. Most people do not realize that they can be the writer, producer, director, and star of their own drama rather than being a bit player in a wiser persons drama.

This lifetime is all about being. It is about the journey, the quest, and the overcoming of negative circumstances. You should be continually evolving, continually learning and being challenged. If you're not doing this you will surely be stuck in a rut, bored, unhappy, and being that bit player in someone else's drama.

The ability that God gave us to create our reality can work both positively and negatively in our lives. You see, He gave us free will to create. He did not say He was going to limit us to positive creations. We can, and most of us do, create negatives in our lives. The more time you spend thinking about something and the more emotion you put behind your thoughts, the faster they will manifest, positive or negative.

There are other factors to consider. It must be for the greater good, you must be willing to accept something different but better and you must be willing to take the necessary steps or sacrifices. For instance, if you want to become a brain surgeon, you must meet society's requirements, which call for hard work and sacrifice while obtaining the proper education.

I've told you can change your life if you build a relationship with God and that you can create both positive and negative reality in your life. How do we start building the relationship and eliminating the negatives? Actually, it is as simple as A-B-C.

One way to start building a relationship with God is to make a list of some attributes you associate with God. God has many attributes, all of them positive, none negative. God is limitless. It is impossible to recognize all that God is , but, and here is the key: if you do not try to recognize the attributes of God you will not know what is possible. God IS, always was and forever will be. However, it is up to you to investigate, to find out what this divine power is and what He offers.

If I asked you to come up with a list of 10 attributes that help describe God most of you would list items like Omnipresent (always present), Omniscient (all knowing), Almighty, Magnificent, Forgiving, etc. Actually, you could probably do this rather quickly without much thought. Also most of those words are not used in your daily vocabulary.

My goal is for you to have to think!

My system requires that you come up with 26 attributes, one for each letter of the alphabet, a great thinking and discovering exercise. What you will be doing is recognizing attributes that God already possesses - you just didn't think about them before. It is important to note that you cannot totally define God. He is limitless and possesses characteristics that our simple minds just cannot fathom.

The process of building your <u>God Is...</u> alphabet should take place over time, perhaps a month, start with any letter. Write down all the words that start with that letter that describe what God means to you. (Pages provided) Meditate on those words and pick one. Then write a description of what this word means to you in relationship with God. This is the start of building a better relationship. It makes you start thinking about what <u>God Is</u> and what He can be in your life. Do this for all 26 letters and you cannot avoid building a relationship and opening the communication channel with God.

How do we use this to eliminate negatives from our life? As I mentioned before, thinking negative thoughts causes them to manifest. Well - eliminate the negative thoughts. Much easier said than done. Negative thoughts can creep back into your mind, into your consciousness very quickly. To eliminate the negatives, recite your God Is... alphabet. It becomes a mantra - a positive chant. You are really accomplishing two things. First, by reciting 26 sentences you're changing the thoughts in your mind for a few moments. Long enough to chase out the negative.

Secondly, and most importantly, you are thinking the most positive thoughts possible. You are calling upon God, calling upon the relationship you have been building. You're taking the negative thought, purging it from your mind with thoughts about God. What could be more positive?

The negatives can creep back in. Treat it again. Negativism is just like a disease. It can occur again, and again. Just like any sickness, you must treat it. Treat it with a positive antidote. Before you know it, the negative will disappear. When it does disappear, and it will, you will have evidence, experience that God is working in your life. You will never turn back. You will tell others and the world will change. Don't use this system only for treating negatives. It helps in almost any situation. Also, don't stop with only 26 words.

The Exercise

To help you get started I have included my God Is… alphabet as a starter.

As you read through my God IS…alphabet, jot down your meaningful words for each letter. After my this section there is space for you to create your own God Is…alphabet.

God is...
All that there is

Everything that exists is a part of the energy that is God. There is nothing that is not God. He is all that there is. God created our souls, our bodies, the air we breathe, the dogs we pet, the sunsets we watch and He created it all from his energy. Everything is part of God.

God is...
A's

God is...
<u>B</u>eauty

You cannot look at anything without seeing the beauty that is God. Look at a plant, an animal, an atom; they all exhibit divine beauty in both form and function. Then consider the way all life forms function together. No one but God could have envisioned the beauty that we experience every day. Unfortunately, we rarely take the time to notice the beauty.

God is...
B's

God is...
<u>C</u>aring

God cares about every living being in the universe. He cares because He is <u>OUR</u> Father, He created us and He is there for us at anytime and at any place. He cares for us so much that He gave us free will to make our own decisions and to choose our own directions in life. When we make a mistake, He is there to help us out of the difficulty. All we have to do is ask.

God is...
C's

God is...
Divine

God is the only divine being. He is the source of all life, the source of the Laws of Being, the source of all inspiration. He is the only God, the One God.

God is...
D's

God is...
Everlasting

God Is. God always was and always will be. There is no before, no after, only now. God is everlasting and we, the children of God, are also everlasting. Additionally, God is everlasting in the sense that he will always be there for you no matter what you may have done. He never gives up on you!

God is...
Es

God is...
Fair

God created each and every one of us and he created us equal in his image. No one is better or worse than anyone else. We all have the same opportunity to live our lives according to laws of being. God does not question what we ask for because you must make your own mistakes and learn your own lessons. He will answer your request, even if what you are requesting is negative. You may not realize you are creating the negatives. It is up to you to learn how to ask, to learn how to create. If you have pain and sorrow in your life don't blame God and say this is unfair. The pain and sorrow is your choice. Ask Him to remove it and He will. What could be more fair?

God is...
F's

God is...
Good

God is good. There is not one bad aspect to God. God does not do bad things to people. He does not cause sickness and despair. We do it. He gave us the power to create our own reality and He lets us create negative circumstances as well as the positive circumstances. If there is something bad in your life, try to figure out why it is there. What are you supposed to learn from this experience? Learn it and ask God to help you change your circumstances. Remember that He is there to help us out of the bad times and to help us enjoy the good times.

God is...
G's

God is...
Happiness

You cannot know God and not experience happiness. If you know that God loves you, and that He is interested in your happiness, how could you be unhappy?

God is...
H's

God is...
Intelligence

God is the source of all intelligence. He will give you intelligence if you ask for it. There is no question that cannot be answered through God's intelligence. Just ask Him the question and He will provide the answer in that voice that speaks to your soul. You must develop the ability to listen to that voice!

God is...
I's

God is...
<u>J</u>oy

God provides us with the Joy of love, the joy of accomplishment, the joy of sharing, the joy of children, and the joy of playing. Without God, there is no joy.

God is...
J's

God is...
<u>K</u>indness

God is the epitome of kindness. He cares about everyone that exists. He will answer your prayers. He is concerned about you and your daily progress. He gives you what you ask for and what you need. He never punishes you.

God is...
K's

God is...
Love

If you were asked to explain God with one word, the best word would be Love. Love is God's greatest gift, his greatest lesson. Love is God's way. Receive God's love into your heart and let that love touch every part of your life. Let his love radiate from your soul to everyone you contact. If we all did that there would be no problems on earth.

God is...
L's

God Is...
Magnificent

God is the most magnificent being that anyone could ever imagine. He is Divine. His intelligence surpasses the combined intellect of the entire world. His power is unlimited. Most important is the fact that His love for us is unlimited.

God is...
M's

God Is...
Near

God is always near to you. He knows who you are and what you are about. He is there at moment's notice to help you, to comfort you, and to love you. All you have to do is ask.

God is...
N's

God Is...
Our Father

God is OUR Father! God is not the father of only the Christians, or only the Jews, or only the white people, or only the Americans. He is the father of everything that has ever lived in the universe. What this means is that we're all created equal and are equal in the sight of God. Every person is the child of God. Which means that every person is your brother. Isn't it time we started treating every person as our brother?

God is...
O's

God is <u>P</u>erfect

God doesn't make mistakes. He made this world for us to live in and He made it work with perfection even down to the most minute detail. <u>Our</u> mistakes are what threaten the future of this earth.

God is...
P's

God Is...
<u>Q</u>ualified

God is qualified to help you with any problem that you could possibly have. There is nothing that He does not know. He is quite simply the most knowledgeable source that exists for anything that you could ever consider. Moreover, He is willing to help you. All you have to do is ask.

God is...
Q's

God Is...
<u>R</u>adiant

God radiates His love to every one of us every minute of every day. It is up to you to understand that He is doing it and to <u>accept</u> His love. Once you understand and accept His love, you too must radiate His love to your brothers.

God is...
R's

God Is...
Spirit

God is not some bearded old man sitting atop some mountain. God is pure spirit, pure energy. Our true self, our soul, is spirit, pure energy. We are created in His image. We are a part of God. We are one with God.

God is...
S's

God Is...
Truth

Truth is a basic concept that we must all understand. Trust your intuition to recognize the truth. Always be truthful because it you're not, you're not harming anyone but yourself. God is truth. The more you know of God the more truth you will find in your life.

God is...
T's

God Is...
Unique

There is only one God. There is no other being that approaches the power, the intelligence, the wisdom and the love of God. Believing in a devil gives power to the notion that there is a competing God. There is no devil other than the one have you have created within yourself. Know that God is God, unique in the universe. Love Him and your life will change forever.

God is...
U's

God Is...
Vigilant

God doesn't take vacations or coffee breaks. He doesn't make you take a number if you need Him. God is there every minute of every day. He is there to help solve your problems, to comfort you in times of sorrow, to help you plan your tomorrows. God is vigilant and you'll always have an open line to Him.

God is...
V's

God Is...
Wisdom

God is the source of all wisdom. He knows everything that was ever was or ever will be. There is no better source to call upon when you need wisdom. His wisdom can become your wisdom just with a simple task of asking Him for it.

God is…
W's

God Is...
X

In mathematics, X stands for the unknown. X is the value you are trying to find. X is the answer to the problem. God has the X value, the unknown ability. We cannot fathom the true ability of God. We cannot quantify God because he is limitless. So remember that whatever the X might be, whatever problem you might have, God has the ability to solve the equation. He knows the answer.

God is...
X's

God Is...
You

God is you. You are God. That doesn't mean that you are a God but that we are one with God. There is no separation, no division. We all are one with God; we are actually a part, or a piece of God. There is a link of spirit or energy between God and each soul in the universe. That link cannot be broken, ever. This is the reason that access to God is unlimited.

God is...
Y's

God Is...
<u>Z</u>eal

Once you know and understand your relationship with God you have a new zeal for life that comes from God. Once you know the truth you can live with zeal and zest that just doesn't exist when you try to live apart from God.

God is...
Z's

Now the rest is up to you...set some time aside each day for 26 days to think about God and your relationship with Him. Complete the exercise and then start using your God Is... alphabet and see how it can change your life.

If you would like to email me I can be reached at michael@themichaelsgroup.org. I am interested in any comments you may have. Also, contact me if you want to purchase single copies or multiple copies for a discussion group project.

God Is...
A

God Is...
B

God Is...
C

God Is...
D

God Is...
E

God Is...
F

God Is...
G

God Is...
H

God Is...
1

God Is...
J

God Is...
K

God Is...
L

God Is...
M

God Is...
N

God Is...
O

God Is...
P

God Is...
Q

God Is...
R

God Is...
S

God Is...
T

God Is...
U

God Is...
V

God Is...
W

God Is...
X

God Is...
Y

God Is...
Z

Now that you are finished with the exercise let's discuss ways of using it.

The premise of the book is to use your God Is.. alphabet to eliminate the negatives in your life, but there are more uses. You can use your God Is... alphabet to supplement your life, to make your life better.

Try these ideas:

In the morning, in that time when you have just awoken, maybe you have not even opened your eyes yet. Silently go through your mantra before you get up. What a positive way to start your day.

Do you have a meeting today? Do you have to make a presentation. Recite your mantra before you go in. Maybe even substitute some different words that are more appropriate to the task. For example, my C is Caring. If I was supposed to give a presentation I would use God Is...Confidence.

Did your kid mess up and you need to have a talk? God Is... Patience.

I think by now you see the point. Reciting 26 sentences about the positive characteristics you have attributed to God cannot be anything but positive. It can start your day right, it can help you deal with any situation you come across in any day.

Imagine what the world would be like if we all had these thoughts.

The Logic of Reincarnation

Have you thought about what happens when you die? Your body will eventually turn to dust. But what happens to your Soul? Where does it go? What does it do? Do you go to heaven? If so, what do you do once you get there? What about all of the things you wanted to do in your lifetime but never got around to? Are those desires gone forever?

Reincarnation… Multiple lifetimes… You either believe in it or you don't. There is no middle ground. It is either true or it is false. You either get one chance at life or you keep coming back.

I believe that those who do not believe in reincarnation haven't given the issue much thought. If you really think about it, reincarnation makes much more sense than just having one lifetime.

I've never heard reincarnation discussed in any church I have attended. Wonder why that is? Power over you? Control?

The first logical assumption is belief in God. If you do not believe in God you can stop now and save yourself reading the rest of this document because it is based upon a belief in God.

It has been said that God created us in His image and that we are all created equal. Let's examine these statements.

He created us in His image: I don't know what God looks like but I do know that we all look different: Man, woman, fat, thin, tall, short, blonde, brunette, black, white, yellow, brown. So, "in His image" must not mean our physical bodies.

We are all created equal: I don't know about you, but I was not born rich, or good looking, or with great physical prowess. So, "created equal" must not refer to our physical circumstances.

Therefore, when God created us "in His image" and "equal" it refers to our Soul, that unique spirit that defines us. God is Spirit. He created us out of Himself. We are each a part of God. Each of us is equal in that creation, none better, none worse, all the same and at the same time unique. Do not confuse being created equal with being born equal. There is a big difference that we will discuss further.

God created our Souls and the Bible says the Soul lives forever or for eternity. Forever! That is a long time, a very long time. It is so long that time does not exist. Forever or eternity are not finite terms, they are infinite. But for illustration lets assume that forever is a line that goes from the earth to the sun. Then lets assume that you take an razor blade and slit that line in the tiniest cut possible. That slit would represent your present life in time. Seems pretty insignificant doesn't it?

What is the ultimate goal of anyone that believes in God? To me, the ultimate goal is to become knowledgeable enough to live in the presence of God. It would seem that one would acquire that knowledge through experience here on earth or maybe someplace else.

If you do not believe in reincarnation then you must believe that you learn all that is necessary to live in the presence of God in one lifetime. To me that is an arrogant assumption. God is the source of intelligence and knows every human experience that has ever happened. Do you really think one lifetime can give you enough knowledge to have an intelligent conversation with God? Then there is the other question; if the Soul lives forever and you only get one chance at life on Earth, what do you do for the rest of eternity? Do you think you sit on a cloud and play a harp from now on? Nothing that boring, I'm sure. One function of a non-incarnate Soul is to help other Souls in their pursuit of life and knowledge.

What kind of knowledge do you think is necessary to live in the presence of God? There is no manual on this but I cannot believe for one second that it is possible to learn all that is necessary in one lifetime. The person that you are can only experience certain aspects of life. For example, a man cannot experience the aspects of being a woman. If your Soul were to help other Souls it would make sense that you had some experience to draw upon. You can only give advice based upon your experience. In a one lifetime scenario your Soul would only be able to advise Souls that were born into similar circumstances. The reason we have multiple lifetimes is to gather the experience required to really help other Souls. Souls accumulate knowledge in the same way people accumulate knowledge, by experience. Experience comes from multiple lifetimes. In the grand scheme of things I think that it is important to experience life as a man, as a woman, rich, poor, powerful, helpless, pretty, ugly, healthy, sickly, Christian, Muslin, Jew, Buddhist, atheist, and all of the combinations and permutations that exist. Otherwise how could you understand what God wants you to learn? It is about perspective. Experience is what gives you perspective. The Soul is conducting these lifetimes to complete the syllabus of the knowledge required to live in the presence of God.

Suppose for a moment that you are in the presence of God and He wants to have a conversation and says to you, "What do you think about war?" And you, who have never been to war because you were born when there were no wars in your lifetime, have to say, "Gee God, I don't really have an opinion on that because I have no experience. Just believing in God is not enough to live in his presence, you have to do some work and the work involves the experiences involved in multiple lifetimes.

I'm sure you will agree that God can do anything, there is nothing beyond God's ability, He is all-powerful. Right? If you believe this then why would you limit Him by believing that He would only give us one chance to learn our lessons? Doesn't it make sense that when he creates a Soul that lasts for eternity, that that Soul would always be learning and trying to improve it's knowledge base? After all, learning is what we do here on Earth. Why would it be different for a Soul?

What is your true nature? Are you a body that lives one lifetime or a Soul that experiences many lifetimes? What came first, the body or the soul? Did God create your body and then put a soul into the body? Or, did God create your soul and allow it inhabit a body? Who is the boss, the body or the Soul? From the above we know that the Soul lives forever. From practical experience we know that the body dies and turns to dust. Therefore it would follow that the Soul is the smarter of the two pieces, the boss, the greater mind. After all, the Soul lives forever. You are not a body that gets a Soul, you are a Soul that decides to inhabit a body. Once that body dies your Soul can inhabit another body. A lifetime is not about what a body does, it is about what a Soul learns.

Some people will dismiss reincarnation and state that all the people who think they lived before were always some sort of King or Caesar, never a slave, never a commoner. I agree that that is silly. If you could remember your past lifetimes you might not get a lot done. You might be afraid to leave the house because you would remember all the times and ways you died before and you would not want to repeat it. However, there are things that can trigger past life memories; a smell, a landscape, etc. Admit it, there have been times when you say, "I've been here before." But you haven't in this lifetime. Have you ever met a person and thought you had known them before? Just how does that happen if you only live once? You have friends in this lifetime and you have friends in the Soul dimension. The people you meet in this lifetime that you think you have met before are your Soul friends, your classmates. A Soul friend can enter into your life to be your Soulmate or to make you turn right at the next corner to meet your Soulmate or to meet your destiny.

Does it make any sense that God would create the Universe and all of the beauty it encompasses and then create highly complex and intelligent Souls that live forever and limit the Soul to only one chance at life? One chance at learning? This just doesn't compute.

I like to use the metaphor of the Soap Opera. Let's say you are an actor and you get a role in a Soap. For a few hours each day you play the role of a different person. Someone very different from you. Different background, education, family, beliefs, problems, opportunities, etc. Over time you would learn from the experiences of this character you are playing. You would expand your own perspectives about life because of this role you are playing.

After you play this character for a while it becomes second nature to you. You are into the character. Acting is more natural and relaxed. In fact at times you might find yourself thinking through the prism of this character. Being the good actor you are you might even pick up an additional role in a different Soap. You will be playing a completely different character in a completely different environment. Again, you will learn through this characters experiences. Pretty soon you may become bored with one of the characters you are playing and reach the decision that you have learned all that you can learn from this drama and you move on to the next one.

This metaphor explains our existence. We are players on an enormous stage of interconnected dramas. As Souls, we we set up lessons that we want to learn and then come into a life, a body, to try to experience those lessons.

Have you ever warned someone or been warned yourself about the consequences of taking a particular action. Nine times out of ten the person warned will pay no attention to the warning. They have to experience it for themselves for the lesson to sink in! Why would it be different for the Soul?

Remember, time does not exist for a Soul, so having multiple lifetimes just makes sense. Many people experience multiple careers in one lifetime and they have multiple interests that drive them. Why would it be different for a Soul? I think that a Soul would want to experience as many lifetimes as possible.

Some people die young. It could be that they never had the chance to achieve anything in their short lifetime. So what lesson could they have learned? I believe that some Souls come into a lifetime only to be a catalyst for another Soul to learn a lesson. One of the toughest lessons that we have to learn is what it is like to lose a loved one. If it is a child it is even more difficult. As difficult as it may be, losing a loved one is a lesson we will all learn. However, they are not gone, it is just the body that is gone. They came into a life, played a role, and left when their part was finished. They are very much alive in the Soul dimension and will be available to play another role in a different lifetime.

People come into your life all the time as catalysts. They come to you to help get in position to learn your important lessons. You may have only one major lesson to learn in your current lifetime. You may live your entire life preparing for the moment when the lesson presents itself. Imagine the preparation required to be one of the people who walked on the Moon. That lesson of seeing Earth from a totally different perspective took a lifetime of preparation to be eligible for that trip. For each of those people there were many people in their lives that turned them left or right, nudged them here or there to continue on the path. We are all the same. We all have those catalysts that come into our lives. It is no accident. They are there because we need the help, because it is part of the drama we have scripted.

Have you ever encountered a drunk in the gutter? We tend to pass these folks off as the dregs of society. Actually it is possible that some of these folks could be very spiritually advanced, on the Soul level, and need only this lesson to advance to another level. What is the lesson here? Part of it would be to see how the rest of the people treat someone that is down and out. Perspective!

Did God create this incredibly rich experiential environment and your highly intelligent and powerful Soul to live only one lifetime where whatever you did or didn't do is the sum total of your experience forever? Or, did God in his perfect way, create a playground for our Souls to experience life to the fullest, to pursue our interests and to develop our Souls until we have learned enough?

There is

No

End